KU-416-636

ABOUT BIOCHEMISTRY

by

ESTHER CHAPMAN

THORSONS PUBLISHERS LIMITED
37/38 MARGARET STREET, LONDON, W.1

First published March 1966

Reprinted March 1969

SBN 7225 0016 5

MADE AND PRINTED IN GREAT BRITAIN BY
THE GARDEN CITY PRESS LIMITED
LETCHWORTH, HERTFORDSHIRE

ABOUT BIOCHEMISTRY

CONTENTS

FOREWORD

In response to a request by the publishers, this 'About' book is offered to the reader with a lively interest in the elements that have formed the earth and human tissues and continue to nourish human function and intelligence.

I am indebted to many sources of information, to text-books, congressional papers, and other factual material which have contributed to the present purpose. The reader is referred to the bibliography for references and suggestions for further reading.

Author

THE EARTH'S ELEMENTS BECOME HUMAN TISSUE CELLS

BIO is a shortened form of the Greek word 'BIOS' meaning life. Biochemistry is therefore the chemistry of living tissues.

It begins with the inorganic materials present in the earth, its atmosphere, and in its waters, and studies their relationships as these compound and are organized into the tissues of plant, animal, and human life.

In MAN, many of these substances are taken in the form of food for his body. First as a foetus drawing on the mother's blood, and then as a child the growing tissues make of this food blood and bone cells, muscle, nerve, and skin. Involved in this complex activity is the release of energy for body-function and the regeneration of worn out tissues. Much of this chemical activity, commensurate with age, continues throughout life.

The human body consists of millions of cells and the intercellular spaces between them. These group together forming tissues which become highly differentiated for the various needs of the body. The cell itself, varying in shape and size depending on its structure and function, consists of a minute amount of living substance, protoplasm, enclosed in a membrane which in some cases may consist of only a few molecules of texture.

The constituents of *protoplasm* are—

Oxygen, Carbon, Hydrogen, Nitrogen, Sulphur, Calcium, Phosphorus, Potassium, Chlorine, Sodium, Magnesium, Iron, Iodine, Silicon, Fluorine, with

7

traces of Copper, Manganese, Zinc, Cobalt, Nickel, Barium, Lithium, etc.

Much research work has demonstrated that these elements as constituents are essential for healthy body structure and function.

The first five are gaseous elements found in the earth's atmosphere. Of the major metals, the average daily requirement is accepted as being 0.68 gram of calcium, 1.32 gram of phosphorus, 0.012 gram of iron. Of iodine the daily need is only 75 *micro*grams, to the merest trace of copper, zinc, cobalt, etc. These values should all be obtained from the daily meals, and those who take a well-balanced mixed diet with a good variety of fresh vegetables and fruit should find these requirements suitably met.* It is usual to find that if the calcium, phosphorus, iron and iodine contents are all good, such a diet has also met the body's need for the other elements which should have compounded in it.

In addition to those referred to, many of the ninety-two elements which are known to exist naturally as constituents of the earth and its waters are probably present in human tissues—since microscopic amounts have most likely entered into the composition of various natural foodstuffs. A number of these have been traced in human tissues but in such minute amounts that detection has had to be by radiographical means. All these constituent elements promote various chemical reactions within the body.

Most of these elements exist in the body as compounds, and very often as highly complex substances. A little free oxygen, hydrogen, and nitrogen are reported to have been found in the blood and intestines, but it is unusual in human tissues to find these elements except as compounds. Those substances which contain carbon are

* See also General Food Requirements, p. 39.

classed as organic compounds, and occur in protoplasm as proteins, carbohydrates, and fats.

The inorganic compounds in human tissues are present either as dissolved salts, or occur in combination with the organic compounds. If this organic matter is burned the mineral elements remain and are therefore also known as ash constituents.

Oxygen has to be present for life as we know it to exist. It is taken on the breath,* stored in the lungs, and taken up by the blood where it compounds with a protein and iron, and to effect this activity copper has to be present: having become haemoglobin it is transported by the blood and lymph to all tissues of the body.

Hydrogen forms two-thirds the volume of water with oxygen as H_2O. Water is the greatest requirement of the human tissues and forms about two-thirds of body weight. It is the most suitable medium in which all material—nutritional and waste products—can circulate in solution. Water has high solvent power for these substances and for high concentrations of them: it has, also, excellent capacities for ionization† of solvent substances, and for conducting heat in liquid form.

The chemical element carbon occurs compounded with oxygen as carbon dioxide, CO_2, and in all organic matter as proteins, carbohydrates, or fats.

Nitrogen, a gas that forms four-fifths of the earth's atmosphere, is taken into the body on the breath and in certain foods, since it is an essential element of all protein.

Sulphur is an essential element in some proteins. It is a constituent of body tissues, notably the hair and the skin. Sulphur tends to balance phosphorus. It is a constituent of nerve tissue and eliminates excessive nerve irritation and excitability: sulphur promotes bile secretion,

* The constituents of the breath (atmospheric air) are oxygen, nitrogen, and carbon dioxide.

† See Values of Ionization, p. 34.

stimulates hair growth, and is a factor in regulating body temperature. Sulphur combined with oxygen occurs as a constituent of cartilage, and in the naturally secreting mucous. In foods it is found in egg-white and in fish. Vitamin B_1 contains sulphur.

Almost all the body's calcium, and much of its phosphorus, is in the bones as calcium phosphate. This compound gives strength and rigidity to the skeleton. Its correct distribution and deposition in the tissues is promoted by the presence of Vitamin D within the tissues. Calcium has a functional relationship with the membranes of cells, the excitability of muscle and heart action, and with normal blood clotting. Additional calcium and phosphorus are needed during pregnancy and lactation, when the diet should be adjusted for these and other requirements.

Phosphorus enters into the composition of nerve sheaths and brain tissue, is predominant in the nuclei of cells, and with calcium is a constituent of glandular tissue. As part of the compound, calcium phosphate, it is a major constituent of the bones and the teeth. Phosphorus is also a catalyst in effecting many metabolic changes and is a constituent of body fluids.

Foods rich in calcium are milk, cheese, eggs, whitebait and sardines, and such fish of which the bones are eaten, and watercress. (One pint of milk gives approximately .68 gram of calcium.) Phosphorus is usually found with calcium in cheese, milk, eggs, fish: meat contains some phosphorus, and most fruit and vegetables have small contents. Cereals, pulse vegetables, and nuts contain largely unassimilable phosphorus.

Potassium occurs in the blood and the muscles, in the glands and all soft tissues. Potassium is lost from the body in the urine, but not through the sweat. The following foods have good potassium content: the protein cheeses such as cheddar; eggs; milk; cod; herring; and most other foods contain a little.

Sodium and chlorine are the chief inorganic elements of blood plasma, forming the salt sodium chloride. This salt is of great importance in the production of the gastric juices for good digestion, and carries in the blood the carbon dioxide *from* the tissues to the lungs where it is exhaled. Sodium and chlorine occur also in the muscles. Further, chlorine is a constituent of connective tissue, and promotes a healthy condition of the gums (a form of connective tissue).

Sodium keeps calcium in solution, promotes alkalinity of the blood and attracts substances into solution. Promotes elasticity, and is a balancing factor against the hardening of ligaments and tendons of muscles; and with calcium in solution it prevents the bones and teeth from becoming brittle.

Sodium (together with a minute amount of uranium—which is found in the water of some districts) should prevent the formation of kidney and gall stones (subject also to moderation in diet factors).

Sufficient sodium and chlorine (as sodium chloride) for human daily needs are found in the salted foods as marketed and in the form of common salt that is usually added in cooking many foods. Where too much sodium collects within the tissues, causing them to hold on to additional amounts of water—showing as oedema—a potassium salt can be substituted for common salt and a 'low-salt diet' followed.

Magnesium has a relationship with nerve tissue, the muscle fibres, and the internal organs. It is closely associated with calcium in bone formation, and is a factor of muscle elasticity : a little is found in the blood. A little magnesium is found in most foods.

Iron, in conjunction with a protein, forms the red blood cells, and in combination with another protein (cytochrome) occurs in all body cells : it is essential to the life processes of all cells, and is a factor in converting food into energy.

Human beings with 70 per cent. or less haemoglobin in the blood are considered anaemic. Most women need 15 mg of iron daily, and men need 12 mg daily: some iron is stored in the liver against the body's needs, but *high intakes of iron over an appreciable period* can be injurious.

Excellent sources of assimilable iron are fresh green vegetables, dried fruits, fresh raspberries, loganberries and peaches, liver, kidney, egg-yolks, turnip tops, watercress.

Iodine is contained in the thyroid gland in the preparation of the thyroid hormone, thyroxin. It is a major element of importance in controlling normal growth and the *rate* of metabolism within the body.

Watercress is an excellent source of iodine, while the water it is grown in naturally contains traces of this element: onions also pick up this element well. Sea fish, and carragheen moss are good sources, and a little will be contained in the drinking water from all areas except where the soil is deficient.

Fluorine is a constituent of the enamel of teeth, the nails, and with calcium enters into bone composition and is a part of glandular structure. Soft teeth, prolapsed organs, indicate a lack of fluorine in food or water: the actual requirement is rather less than one part per million.

Silicon in chemical terms is a minute cation around which are four oxygen anions, producing a strong electrostatic force. It easily builds up into compounds, giving these its characteristic flexibility and strength (seen in the long fine stalks of grasses). It readily forms carbonates—a valuable buffer substance in the blood—or combines again to form a salt, silica, with ionizing properties in the tissues. In forming carbonates it gives off carbon dioxide, which is duly eliminated from the lungs.

Silicon is a constituent of all connective tissue, the hair, the nails, the outer layer of the skin and the eye, without which these tissue cells would become soft and spongy.

Copper vitalizes movement within the tissues, reducing static and inflammatory conditions by promoting magnetic-electric flow. It carries oxygen, promoting oxidation, and is a good conductor of body temperature. Reduced elastic tissue content of the aorta is one of the primary symptoms of copper deficiency: other effects of a deficiency are decreased growth and anaemia, in which it reflects its essential factor in forming haemoglobin. Copper is an essential element also of certain enzymes which cannot oxidize without it.

Many foods contain minute amounts of copper, particularly green peas, cocoa powder, and chocolate, butter beans, and Brazil nuts.

Manganese acts as a catalyst in the reduction of food products to simple substances: it is found in the cerebrospinal fluid and in the blood.

Zinc is a constituent of insulin. It is found in the red corpuscles of the blood and in the lining cells of the stomach: it has a connection with normal growth and development. Zinc may have some relationship with the male sex glands, since high concentrations occur normally in sperms, seminal fluid, and in the prostate gland.

Cobalt contains a protein and is associated with digestive processes: it is part of Vitamin B_{12}. If this element is not contained in the diet, anaemias develop. It is known to occur in liver, fermentation liquors, and milk.

Minute quantities of manganese, boron, and other elements apparently needed in body metabolism are usually found in food produce and drinking water unless the locality shows a soil deficiency of one or several of these elements.

The essential elements of carbohydrates are carbon, hydrogen, and oxygen: these same elements occur in fats, but in different and rather complex combinations. Those of protein are carbon, hydrogen, oxygen, nitrogen, and very often sulphur.

DESCRIPTION OF BODY STRUCTURES

The total living substance within each cell, the protoplasm, consists of a nucleus—again within an enclosing membrane—and its surrounding cytoplasm. The structure of the cytoplasm varies considerably in different cells depending on their functions. Inherent in the nucleus is the ability to produce chemical change, on which all cell activity depends.

The metabolism, or life activity, of each cell involves the ingestion of its nutrient material and its conversion to the cell's own substance and requirements for its growth and reproduction, which is anabolic activity: and in turn the breakdown of that resultant material for elimination after it has served its purpose and ended its particular life cycle—a catabolic activity.

These chemical activities are increased by warmth and by various stimuli.

In absorbing oxygen some part of the cell structure is oxidized,* liberating energy. Carbon dioxide is thus formed; a minute amount is used in metabolic activity and the excess is eliminated. This process is also called cellular respiration.

Every living cell has the property of irritability, which enables it to respond to stimuli. This is conducted throughout the protoplasm, which is then termed excited. If the stimuli is one of lessened activity, the cell irritability is inhibited. Protoplasm has the ability to

* The oxidation–reduction process is referred to more fully see p. 29.

contract, and to stream within the cell membrane and to carry substances from one part of the cell to another, giving it the activities of motion and circulation.

Some epithelial cells have developed and project microscopic processes called cilia, which possess a whipping or ciliary movement to propel secretions along their surfaces and prevent the entry of unwanted organisms. This is a feature of the epithelial tissue of the respiratory tract from the nose to the lungs.

The actual form the cell takes depends partly on pressure from surrounding tissue, the character of its contents and its differentiation, its movement, its growth. Its chemical composition is immediately related to its function, which is first to effect those activities essential for its own life to continue, and to contribute to the activity of tissue structure of which it is part.

The tissues of the human body are grouped into connective tissue, muscular tissue, nerve tissue, and epithelial tissue.

In connective tissue the cells contain relatively few elements, but there is much substance in the intercellular spaces, which show considerable variation and this is governed by its function in the body. Connective tissue supports as well as connects other structures of the body.

In this group are included the primary aerolar tissue, the blood and lymph systems, the neuroglia which is connective in function and carries the nerve stimuli (but is considered separately as nerve tissue), cartilage—a form of fibrous connective tissue which covers the end of bones —and the bones which are specialized and hardened connective tissue.

Aerolar tissue is a network of cells and semifluid matrix, connecting and insulating all tissues. It is continuous throughout the body, underlying the skin and the mucous membranes, and is part of the tissue structure of blood vessels, nerves, organs. Because of this continuity, an infection easily spreads from one site to other parts of the body. Adequate supplies of Vitamin A, which has a protective function for all connective tissue, if taken in the daily diet should strengthen the resistance of these tissues against infections. Since aerolar tissue insulates the deeper structures and organs good resistance should prevent the penetration of an external infection.

If aerolar tissue cells become filled with fat it is referred to as adipose tissue, when it has the additional functions of reducing heat loss and providing a food reserve for later energy production. But good elimination of fatty deposits through the lymph vessels best contributes to healthy function.

The blood consists of cells floating in an intercellular liquid called plasma. This fluid, approximately nine-tenths of which is water, contains many complex substances since it carries all the essential nutrition to every part and cell of the body and carries away in the process of elimination the waste products of continual cell activity. It is slightly alkaline in reaction.

The blood acts then as a transporting medium for endocrine secretions, the enzymes, hormones, the inorganic salts derived from the breakdown and assimilation of food and from the chemical reactions of body metabolism, its own manufactured antibodies, and the small amounts of dissolved gases previously referred to.

The blood cells consist of the red cells—an elastic framework which contains the haemoglobin carrying iron and oxygen to all tissues, the white cells with ameboid or 'wandering' movement which ingest bacteria at pathological sites, and thrombocytes which supply coagulant material.

The material circulating in the blood, in solution, is diffused through the membranes of the blood walls into the lymph channels or intercellular spaces (with the exception of those cells lining the blood vessel walls which are directly in contact with the blood).

In the course of blood circulation and lymph diffusion all cells draw in to themselves those substances in solution they need for their own cell life, and by a dual process they eliminate their used material as chemical by-products which, in solution, are returned by the lymph to the blood.

Lymph is the intermediary infiltration of blood plasma to the tissue cells, diffusing blood nutrients, and inter-changing waste products from these cells to the blood. Lymph fills the intercellular spaces throughout the body, the serous cavities, and the synovial fluids, the fluids of the bursae: it forms the endolymph and the perilymph of the internal ears, the fluids of the eyes: cerebrospinal fluid can be classed as lymph.

Lymph has of course a higher content of waste products than the blood and a lower nutritional content: both circulations are variable in different parts of the body because of specific tissue requirements and waste return, but both are almost constantly stable in total.

The skeletal bones develop from foetal cartilage, those of the skull from membranous tissue. The intercellular spaces of this connective tissue become specifically hardened with deposits of mineral salts, and finally constitutes about two-thirds of its weight. The mineral salts are—

Calcium phosphate	...	...	approx. 58%
Calcium carbonate	...	...	„ 7%
Calcium fluoride ...	...	...	„ 1–2%
Magnesium phosphate	...	...	„ 1–2%
Sodium chloride ...	...	...	less than 1%

The cells, blood vessels, and gelatinous matter, these organic constituents approximate 33 per cent.

Growth of bone and its correct ossification depend on the absorption of sufficient calcium and phosphorus from the daily food, together with certain chemical substances, principally Vitamin D and the autacoid thyroxine secreted by the thyroid.

Muscle tissue forms another group. The cells forming this tissue are elongated and are highly developed for the properties of contractility, extensibility, and elasticity, enabling the tissue to change its shape and to return to its original form when the stimulus is removed, giving these tissues the function of movement. A small amount of physiological cement in the intercellular spaces holds the muscle cell to its framework of connective tissue.

A third group consists of nerve tissue formed by nerve cells and their numerous connective processes, some reaching great length and extending from one part of the body to another. These cell bodies are also composed of cytoplasm and a nucleus. In the cytoplasm, including that of the nerve processes, are found neurofibrils. The final axons or nerve endings consist almost wholly of neurofibrils. The cytoplasm contains a chromophilic substance : the amount varies and is lessened in conditions of fatigue, fever, injury, and conditions of toxaemia.

Nerve cells, or neurons, possess a distinct polarity for nerve impulses and their function is to transmit these to their axons and the responsive tissue in which these terminate.

Nerve tissue forms into two interactive nervous systems. The autonomic system regulates and controls such activities as the contractions of the stomach, intestinal peristalsis, the automatic contraction and relaxation of the heart muscle, and the output of glandular secretions. The cerebrospinal or voluntary nervous system is concerned with consciousness, with mental activity, and the use of the skeletal muscles in voluntary movements.

The other group of tissue is called epithelial. It is composed of closely packed cells with only the minimum of intercellular substance, and is held together largely by a cell cement. It forms surface boundaries of protective tissue, usually in the nature of a membrane, and is nourished by the lymph through its intercellular spaces.

The cells reproduce continuously and push their older, partly used prototypes outwards, which then become rubbed off and are easily eliminated.

Where epithelial tissue forms a layer of smooth lining cells it secretes a fluid, serum, to lubricate any movement and avoid friction as in lining the alveoli of the lungs, the lens of the eye, the tissues of the inner ear.

A membrane is an expansion of thin tissue and usually consists of a layer of epithelial tissue overlying a layer of connective or other tissue.

A gland is a group of cells whose functional purpose is to manufacture specific substances *from blood constituents and lymph* for secretion outside themselves. These secretions, such as the digestive fluids, the lacrimal and mammary glands, contain enzymes. These act as catalyzers, varying the rate of chemical reactions and are specific to the medium. For example, pepsin requires an acid medium : proteins are digested by trypsin in an alkaline or a neutral solution and cannot react in free acid. These enzymes are most effective at optimum body temperature. Certain of these enzymes require activating by a second substance. Both inorganic and organic substances activate various but specific enzymes, the former are called activators, and the latter kinases. The amount produced of the specific secretion is affected both by nervous and chemical stimuli.

Endocrine glands secrete directly into the blood and lymph : *exocrine* glands secrete into a body cavity or on to its surface.

All glands and glandular tissue secrete chemical products known as autacoids (Greek for natural remedy). Certain of these *stimulate* metabolic function and are called hormones. Those that *inhibit* (or make slack) metabolic activities are called chalones. Autacoids are secreted into the circulatory fluids. Control of output of the autacoids is linked with the pituitary body and the nervous system through the hypothalamus.

The organs of the body are each a unit of tissue structures specially adapted and organized to perform a particular function in the body. The organ is part of and shares in the work of a body-system.

The brain is the central organ of the nervous system, consisting of a complexity of nerve tissue organized for receiving, sorting, collecting and transmitting sensation, evoking and directing thought, by the discharge of nervous energy. Its interior fibres link parts of the brain together and connects it with the spinal cord, from which the spinal nerves emerge in pairs and connect to all parts of the trunk and limbs.

The organs of sight and hearing are intricately developed tissue structures, containing, protecting, and nourishing the sensory end-organs of the cranial nerves elaborated for these activities.

The heart, a hollow muscle supplied with blood vessels and nerves, valves and fibrous connective tissue, is the central organ of the circulatory system, and pumps the blood through its arteries and capillaries to all parts of the body. And by diffusion, the blood nutrients enter the supplementary lymphatic system and are drawn across the cell membrane to nourish the cell contents.

The reverse process of waste is gathered from the cell by the lymphatic intermediary system and returned to the veins; here, by means of valves and body pressure venous blood enters the inferior and superior venae cavae and then the right atrium of the heart, where it is conducted to the right ventricle and the pulmonary artery for re-oxygenation by the lungs. Later, it is re-gathered from the lungs by the pulmonary veins to the left side of the heart, through the left atrium and the left ventricle to enter the aorta and re-take its circulation to all body tissues.

The respiratory system for supplying the body with oxygen and eliminating most of its carbon dioxide centres on the lungs, a pair of lobes each consisting of many lobules. Each lobule is penetrated by a bronchiole and blood supply. The bronchioles give off air cells, or alveoli, approximately 700,000,000 in all, which aerate the blood brought for oxygenation. The nasal cavities first filter the incoming air, and the pharynx transmits it to the larynx and the trachea, through which air reaches the bronchial tubes to the lungs.

The alimentary system begins with the mouth—the tongue, teeth, salivary glands—and assisted by the pharynx the food is conducted to the oesophagus away from the trachea,* and continuing through the organs of digestion, the stomach, the duodenum, and the small intestine with its four to five million villi (finger-like little glands that line its length and through which the digested material is absorbed into the blood).

The pancreas and the gall bladder are important assistant organs of digestion in secreting digestive juices into the duodenum.

And after absorption, the remaining waste matter passes on to the colon—ascending, transverse, and descending, according to its location, before it reaches the rectum and the waste material is eliminated as faeces.

The liver is a highly composite organ, since it acts as a storehouse for various blood materials; it secretes bile, and in this belongs to the digestive system; and receives certain body wastes for further destruction and elimination and is in some measure part of the excretory system.

It transforms such substances as glucose from carbohydrates into glycogen and stores it, together with iron and copper : its enzymes reconvert these substances and re-admit them when required by the blood for circulation. As well, the liver rids the body of poisonous by-products of chemical activity which it secrets into the bile for elimination, and regulates the various concentrations of amino acids in the blood from its conversion of these

* Also known as the windpipe which leads to the bronchi and the lungs.

acids into glucose and urea, which latter is then eliminated by the kidneys, passed down the ureters and into the bladder for voiding.

The spleen, a lymph gland is an adjunct to the liver in its function of the destruction of aged cells, and acts also as a reservoir of blood cells for emergency needs, such as those of emotional stress and hard physical exercise: and it is possibly the place of origin of new blood cells after conditions of anaemia. Its position is behind the stomach and to the left of it.

It is probable that the function of the thymus gland which lies against the trachea is largely concerned with antibody formation in the young. In later life it usually atrophies.

The thyroid gland lying across the trachea controls normal growth and development in the young, and the metabolic rate of the body: this latter affects the heart's beat, oxidation, and is a factor in the elimination of nitrogen.

The parathyroids secrete a hormone which maintains calcium levels in the blood, and the irritability (correct excitation) of the nervous system and the muscles.

The adrenals or suprarenal glands (one above the upper end of each kidney) secrete the hormone epinephrine (also called adrenaline) and promote muscular tone. Increased secretion of adrenaline is the immediate response to an emotional or physical emergency, with a rise in general blood pressure and equipment for muscular activity: the fight or flight reaction.

The pituitary, situated in the sella turcica deep within the skull, appears to have the controlling function of the ductless glands, though it is also thought that certain of the relative nerve impulses originate within the thalamus itself or in the floor of the brain. Pituitary function is related to normal growth and to the normal development of the reproductive system.

The human reproductive system consists, in the male,

of the two testes with seminal vesicles and ducts enclosed in the scrotum, the penis and prostate gland, the seminal fluid and the spermatozoa, and the relevant nerve fibres controlling ejaculation. In the female are the two ovaries, which produce the ova and the ovarian secretions (theelin and progesterone), the fallopian tubes, the uterus and uterine tubes, the vagina and external genitals, and the breasts.

A new life comes into existence by the union of two cells, one of which is produced by the male—a mature spermatozoa—and the other by the female, an ova.

The tissues of these organs and systems have to be supplied with their own nutrient material necessary for the health of their own continuing life and for their function in the body. Every part is concerned in the metabolism of the whole body : it is acted upon, and reacts as part of a unit. Every chemical activity is interactive with another, and the energy thus released is being continually translated.

A. THE DIGESTION AND ABSORPTION OF FOOD

The life chemistry of the human body depends on its intake of food for its continuing activity. This food has to be absorbed into the blood and circulated to all body tissues by a chain of digestive processes. These processes gradually reduce complex foods—the carbohydrates into simple sugars, the fats into glycerin and fatty acids, the proteins into amino acids, together with the inorganic substances and vitamins that these compounds contain, into a soluble form that is permeable through cell membranes.

These digestive processes involve both mechanical and chemical factors.

An attractive display of food, its odour and taste stimulate nerve endings and increase digestive secretions. In its preparation and cooking, certain digestive processes have been initiated: cellulose is softened and broken up, the starch of carbohydrates has been changed to dextrin, fats are partially split up, and the first stages of some protein decomposition are effected. And the cooking process kills some harmful organisms which might interfere with effective digestion.

The body's mechanical digestive processes commence with mastication and deglutition, continuing with the peristalsis of the oesophagus, the movements of the stomach and of the intestines and finishing with the excretory processes.

Chemical digestive processes within the body are controlled by the autonomic nervous system which innervates the tissues of the digestive organs, the heart, and the glands. But nervous strain, unpleasant emotion, conditions of stress, stimulate the adrenal glands to pour adrenaline into the blood, preparatory to muscular exertion for fight or flight, and all such conditions as these are inhibitory to digestive secretion.

The hydrolysis* of chemical digestion is dependent upon the presence of enzymes, specific to its substance and medium. There are the starch-splitting enzymes called amylases in the saliva; the protein-splitting enzymes called proteinases, such as pepsin of the gastric fluid; the sugar-splitting enzymes, e.g. maltase which splits maltose into dextrose, and others which split glucose of the tissues into lactic acid; and in the pancreatic secretion, fat-splitting enzymes called lipases. In addition, there are clotting enzymes such as rennin, and others which cause oxidation.

Mastication and salivation occur together. The saliva is composed mostly of water and, in solution, some mucin for lubrication purposes, inorganic salts, some protein material, and the enzyme ptyalin or salivary amylase.

The changing of starch into dextrin and maltose is effected in a number of stages *beginning* with the ptyalin of the saliva—which should be nearly neutral in reaction. An acid saliva hinders this process.

On entering the stomach, food is held there and subjected to rhythmic contractions—increasing in strength towards the pyloric end—which macerate it and mix it with the acid gastric fluid, reducing it to a thin liquid chyme. Periodically, part of the chyme reaches a degree of acidity and fluidity which relaxes the pyloric sphincter and allows the chyme to pass into the duodenum. But its acidity there causes the pyloric sphincter to contract again, and the chyme is thus prevented from flowing

* The splitting of complex molecules into simpler ones with the absorption of water.

back to the stomach but is subjected to intestinal activity.

Gastric juice is secreted constantly : this is increased while eating, and during the digestion of food.

Some food substances, notably meat juices, yield hormones which it is considered stimulate the nerves of the digestive tract to produce gastrin—which in turn stimulates the gastric glands to secrete. Other foods which do not contain these hormones, such as milk and bread, these on being eaten apparently initiate certain digestive processes which, in turn, stimulate increased gastric secretion. Different stimuli appear to be involved with different foods, but the effect on metabolism is to increase gastric and intestinal secretions.

The consumption of fats tends to lower gastric secretion.

The gastric fluid secreted in the stomach consists chiefly of mucin, inorganic salts and some protein, but the essential constituents are hydrochloric acid and the enzymes, pepsin, rennin, and lipase. It is thought that the hydrochloric acid is formed from sodium chloride circulating in the blood.

Delayed gastric digestion may occasion fermentation of the sugars : this produces gas, and distress from this condition is not uncommon.

The function of hydrochloric acid is to activate the pepsinogen and produce pepsin, to provide an acid medium for this enzyme, to act as a disinfectant on any organisms in the stomach, and to assist in controlling the pyloric sphincter : hydrochloric acid has also a preliminary action on protein fibres and cane sugars.

Some degree of fermentation is natural in the stomach and produces lactic acid, which with the action of the hydrochloric acid results in a chyme of acid reaction now entering the duodenum.

The pancreas is a composite gland situated behind the stomach. It secretes its fluids, together with that from the bile duct, into the duodenum and this composite secretion contains those enzymes which act on carbohydrates, proteins, and fats.

The greatest digestive changes occur in the intestines. The partly digested food, as chyme, is here mixed with the pancreatic fluid and with the alkaline intestinal secretion containing sodium carbonate and several enzymes, and the hormone secretin. It is also subjected to muscular peristalsis and to the presence of bile—which assists in splitting the fats. Carbohydrates and proteins continue to be hydrolysized: the peptids are reduced to amino acids, the maltose and dextrin become dextrose, and the disaccharides are reduced to simple sugars.

Normally, organisms of the small intestine effect a fermentation of the carbohydrates present, and this is a factor in avoiding putrefaction of protein until it enters the large intestine, or colon. The process of digestion and the absorption of food continues (with the enzymes contained in it) in the large intestine, and now occurs the putrefaction of any undigested protein. Some of these unabsorbed products form into the faeces and are periodically expelled through the rectum, and others are carried to the liver, processed still further and finally excreted through the urine.

B. CHEMICAL ACTIVITIES WITHIN HUMAN TISSUES

Body metabolism includes all those processes of chemical activity which enables the creature to live and function. Metabolism includes the intake of air, the digestion of food, the absorption of the resultant nutrient material and the elimination of waste in the excretions; the functioning of its nervous system, the response and reaction to internal secretions and to outside stimuli, and to the processes of conscious thought and personal feeling.

Metabolic processes are promoted by the availability of oxygen within the tissues (taken up from the lungs and circulated by the blood), by enzymes formed within the tissues which act as catalysts, by the hormones which stimulate chemical activities, the Vitamins as accessory food factors, and the inorganic mineral elements which function as ions (having conductive power).

As well, the conversion of organic foods into simple assimilable nutrients, and the continual activities of the body's autonomic nervous system both utilize and promote metabolic processes.

Basal metabolism refers to the units of energy, Calories, that are necessary to keep the body alive. These are influenced by sex, age, daily activities, internal secretions, and emotional intensity. The activity of sleep uses 65 Calories per hour, that of light exercise 170 per hour, office work 170 per hour, sitting and resting uses 100 Calories per hour, and the overall digestion of the whole day's food uses approximately 200 Calories—depending on the type and quantity of food eaten.*

The term 'nutritional needs' covers the requirement for keeping the lymph supplied with the various nutrients and in the correct concentrations needed for the individual cells. Sufficient Calories must be supplied for the requirements of basal metabolism, all muscular activities, and changing temperature. The Calories supplied must also provide in a variety of food substances all 'nutritional needs'—the amino acids, simple sugars, glycerin, essential fatty acids, inorganic elements, Vitamins, and water.*

The metabolism of carbohydrates reduces these into simple sugars, and after absorption through the intestinal capillaries these are stored in the liver, where they become glycogen and are released into the blood and muscle tissue as and when required both for energy and

* See also General Food Requirements, p. 39.

to maintain body temperature : excess sugar is a factor of adipose tissue.

Fats are split into glycerin and fatty acids, and when oxidized supply energy for cell processes. When these fatty substances are needed by the cells they are absorbed from the blood.

Protein metabolism brings these substances down to amino acids which re-enter the general circulation : the tissues then select and use certain of these circulating substances to build new tissue or to repair metabolism waste.

THE OXIDATION PROCESS

Few substances have sufficient chemical attraction for each other as to cause spontaneous combination. And such reactions would ordinarily be too slight to be of use within human tissues for promoting the numerous essential metabolic activities. The process of combination is however 'touched off' by several agencies. The chief of these is the water in the tissue cells and the intercellular spaces. When substances are put into solution, an even dispersal of their particles is effected and re-combinations are more easily achieved.

Warmth generates chemical changes that otherwise remain inert at lower temperatures, and the body's blood-heat is a promoting factor.

Catalysts 'touch off' many chemical changes within body tissues which otherwise require high temperatures to effect this process. (Certain of these catalysts, those that are themselves formed within the living cell, usually a protein substance, are called enzymes.)

Water, and oxygen, can each act as a catalyst in some cases, achieving chemical change and dissolution. Certain of the Vitamins assist catalytic processes.

Certain elements combine with oxygen with great facility—hydrogen, carbon, and sulphur, have this chemical affinity—at the same time 'reducing' or causing other substances into de-composition by taking oxygen from them.

This oxidative process is most active in the human body in breaking down into simpler substances the food products ingested. The whole digestive process consists of a long chain of oxidative and other chemical activities, each releasing units of energy to the body for use and as these are needed.

These food products contain the elements carbon, hydrogen, and oxygen. *Within the body* the carbon quickly combines with oxygen, forming carbon dioxide and reducing the original substance in doing so; hydrogen immediately compounds with oxygen to form water, a reduction at the same time of the original substance. Both immediate chemical activities are oxidative processes.

The operating oxygen has come from the air and been taken on the breath : it has been brought into the circulation with the iron in the haemoglobin, with which oxygen has another chemical affinity, and another oxidative process is effected.

OSMOSIS

The molecules of a solution will pass from this medium to a more dilute solution, or to pure water, through a permeable membrane lying between the two fluids. Such a membrane may be permeable only for certain molecules in the solution and semi-permeable for others. Inorganic salts are diffusible into living tissues since their membranes are permeable to these salts : other substances such as sugar are not.

Within living tissues there also exists a *selective* flow of such material through the membranes of cells to and from the intercellular spaces. This process is known as *osmosis*, and the pressure so established is called osmotic pressure. This is uniform in general throughout the body, though being continuously variable locally.

Thus, if a more concentrated solution lies in the intercellular space than that of the cell contents immediate to it, diffusion will move from the intercellular space into the cell. Once the higher concentration has moved to the cell contents, osmosis is exerted in the opposite direction, and a general equilibrium is thus maintained. In this way any unsuitable concentration automatically tends to be reduced.

Osmosis within living tissues does not, however, function quite so automatically as in laboratory tests and exercises, since other factors are also operative. The chief of these is that living organs have the power to absorb selectively those substances they need, taking larger amounts of one substance than another from the concentration being presented to the permeable membrane.

The two elements having the chief influence on body fluids and osmotic pressure are sodium and potassium.

Sodium salts are strongest in the intercellular spaces, and potassium ions occur more abundantly within the cells. These are also two of the most chemically active elements. Sodium is a very free element and does not compound into complex organic substances : it is specially important in the regulation of acid-base balance of body fluids.

Potassium occurs in the striated muscle cells and the red blood cells as 200 parts per 100,000 : potassium also assists in maintaining the correct acid-base balance.

Diffusible chloride, when found in association with sodium and potassium, also becomes a factor in osmosis : in this association it is found in glandular tissues and in submucous connective tissue.

FROM THE ELEMENTS TO THE NUTRIENT SALTS

'Energy can be neither created nor destroyed although it can be transformed from one form to another.'

'A chemical change is one in which the composition of the substance is altered, resulting in the formation of one or more new substances with different properties.'

'Matter can neither be created nor destroyed, although it can be changed from one form into another.'

From L. Jean Bogert's *Fundamentals of Chemistry*.

The earth's matter, including that of its seas and its atmosphere, consists of elements. These elements may be gases, solids, or liquids. All elements have distinctive chemical properties. They are classed as metals, for example copper, calcium, gold, iron, lead, potassium, sodium, etc., or non-metals such as carbon, iodine, oxygen, phosphorus, silicon, sulphur, etc. Metals easily conduct heat and electricity : non-metals do not.

All elements consist of a common substance, being aggregations of positive and negative electrical units. Elements differ one from another only in the number of these units that each contains, and in the arrangement of such units that comprises their structure.

The chemical character of an element is its ability to combine with other elements, known as its valence. Such combinations are more easily effected between those of opposite character, and each in doing so tends to become more stable in its structure.

An element is made up of molecules, the atoms of which are of the same sort, e.g. oxygen consists of two atoms of the same character equally tied $o = o$: ozone consists of three same atoms loosely tied, cohering in a triangular form and therefore more easily decomposed.

On combining with another element, one or more of its molecules are displaced, altering its structure and chemical nature.

(Note: There are six elements, the inert gases, whose structure is so stable that their outer orbits of atoms show no tendency to enter into any combinations.)

Metals and hydrogen, considered as being positive elements are made up of atoms that easily lose electrons from their outer orbits and inherently attract the non-metals (considered as the negative elements) which are made up of atoms whose structure thus becomes more stable by taking on extra 'positive' electrons.

All elements have to enter into any such combinations as will give the compound an equal number of positive and negative charges, rendering the compound molecule electrically neutral.

There are four main groups of inorganic compounds —oxides, acids, bases, salts.

Oxides are all substances containing one element in combination with oxygen. Compounds of non-metals with oxygen are called acidic oxides, and these form *acids* when dissolved in water.

Bases are metallic compounds made up of a metallic element with one atom of oxygen and one atom of hydrogen intimately associated and acting as a single element.

Bases react with acids and form SALTS. (Silicon, for example, a non-metal reacting in solution first forms silicic acid and reacts again to form the salt, silica.)

A salt is also formed by the union of an acid with a metal and the consequent displacement of hydrogen.

A readjustment of chemical energy takes place every time a chemical change is effected.

Inorganic compounds—acids, bases, and salts—dissolve into separate particles or molecules in water solutions and are then chemically reactive. Since they carry their electrical charge, they are known as ions. These ions contain an equal number of positive and negative electrons and the solution thus carries a neutral charge.

Organic compounds enter chemical reactions but are much slower to do so than inorganic compounds.

It is usual to find that SALTS provide *high ionization*. A greater degree of solution to the salt gives a higher and more effective ionization (i.e. more solution allows greater freedom of movement to the ions so that they do not so easily collide and then immediately reform a combination). This factor has importance in using specific salts in very fine dilutions for micro-nutrient purposes.

THE VALUE OF IONIZATION WITHIN HUMAN TISSUES

'Ions are electrically charged particles into which molecules of certain chemicals (especially salts, acids and bases) are dissociated by solution in water, and which make such a solution a conductor of electricity. A similarly charged molecule of gas occurs in air.'

Oxford Dictionary

Ionization promotes the electro-magnetic potential of the cell contents and the intercellular fluids—in effect stimulating the cell contents to full vitality.

Many inorganic minerals, it will be remembered, exist in human tissues : mostly, these have entered into combinations and become chemical salts. They occur in body fluids—the blood and lymph—and in the cell protoplasm, much of which is water which ionizes their particles—or molecules.

As ions the chemical activity of these molecules is much more effective. The correct acidity of the gastric juice is due to hydrogen ions from the hydrochloric acid present : further, the accompanying enzymes require a certain degree of hydrogen-ion concentration to effect gastric digestion.

The intestinal alkalinity is effected by the presence of ions formed by sodium carbonates in solution.

The essential degree of alkalinity of the blood is effected by chemical interaction (which in the tissues has produced ionization). The same activity controls the level of water in the tissues and its withdrawal (osmotic pressure).

Many of the organic substances, such as the sugars in plant life, are built up from ionized molecules. This is easily appreciated since plant tissues have high water content.

Fats and proteins—depending on their structures—in process of digestion in body solutions are broken down into particles and many of these molecules are ionizable.

Plant life used for human food, particularly many fruits and vegetables, presents ionized substances which readily return to ions on entering the digestive tract of the human body.

USES OF INORGANIC SALTS IN HUMAN TISSUES

The presence of inorganic salts in body fluids provides a suitable solution for otherwise insoluble substances —certain proteins—needing to be transported to various body tissues, and one also in which uric acid becomes neutralized (to sodium or potassium urates).

Ionization of fluids by these salts—chiefly calcium, potassium, and sodium chloride—provides the correct solution also in which nerves and muscles have to be constantly bathed, and without which the nerve loses its ability to conduct a stimulus and the muscle its ability to contract.

The effects of such ionization on the heart muscle have been fully demonstrated. Calcium salts cause increased contraction: sodium and potassium salts induce greater relaxation. In normal life the heart alternately contracts and relaxes: this condition is partly effected by the calcium salts present in its tissues and partly by the correct proportion of calcium, potassium, sodium and magnesium salts in the body fluids.

(Note: 'Magnesium ions tend to cause relaxation of muscle and depression of the central nervous system'.)

The correct osmotic pressure in the body is largely controlled by the inorganic salts in body fluids, osmotic pressure allowing a selective flow to the cells from the lymph, and in the material being excreted from the cells to the lymph. An insufficiency of certain of these salts in the fluids would allow the cells in many cases to become suffused with water, causing oedema.

Pure proteins, carbohydrates, and fats—the organic elements—supply the body with only five of its twelve major elements. The remainder, the inorganic elements have also to be supplied. Many foods contain inorganic substances within their tissues.

To obtain adequate supplies of organic food and these essential inorganic elements the *daily* diet should contain milk, eggs, cheese, whole grains, fruit, and vegetables.

A high intake of inorganic elements is specially needed by the young to promote correct development and optimum growth; in pregnancy to balance the diet and as a factor in ensuring normal reproduction; in lactation when the mother's diet is fully reflected in her milk for the suckling infant; during convalescence, and particularly where there is much debility and wasting, the inorganic elements promote quick repair of tissue.

Throughout life a reasonably balanced diet that includes adequate inorganic elements should result in a strong constitution in the adult.

If large amounts of urine are passed, or after profuse and continued sweating, small amounts of sodium chloride should be taken to replace the inevitable loss from the body this has occasioned.

Similarly, a considerable loss of blood from any cause will most probably need iron replacement: if calcium has been drawn on—as it is by the foetus in pregnancy—or if a condition of calcium deficiency has been present, this should be made up in the diet, or by specific administration, as soon as possible.

Inorganic salts, chiefly sodium and chlorine, provide the acidity and alkalinity of digestive secretions, producing the correct acidity for the enzyme pepsin to activate digestion of carbohydrates, and an alkaline reaction for the intestinal enzymes and the digestion of proteins and fats.

The cell life of the human body and its metabolism has optimum function in an almost neutral medium, though slightly alkaline. In the processes of metabolism and digestion acids are constantly being formed—carbonic acid from carbon (as carbon oxidizes with oxygen and hydrogen), phosphoric acid from phosphorus. Such acids are injurious to body tissues and are normally promptly neutralized by the elements sodium, potassium, calcium, and magnesium to form salts and water.

Against the event of rather more base or rather more acid concentrations forming, the body has a number of protective factors which normally maintain the overall reaction as almost neutral.

The two chief are a reserve supply of carbon dioxide (an acid forming substance), and an emergency supply of ammonia (a base forming substance). While neutrality continues, the excess supply of carbon dioxide is given off by the lungs, and the ammonia proceeds to compound into urea and is excreted in the urine. As well, some of the excess acid or base will combine with the carbonic acid or ammonia to form the neutral salts.

Again, there are substances in the blood, the phosphates and carbonates, which can combine variously as need arises so that the normal reaction of the blood remains constant.

Should there be a breakdown in the metabolism of any of these protective factors, an abnormal condition arises and disease ensues.

SECTION V

GENERAL FOOD REQUIREMENTS

Much has been written about food and the substances it should contain for good nutrition.

The subject necessarily includes good husbandry of the soil, by which its natural elements having been taken up and synthesized into plant and animal life as food produce are later periodically returned to it as compost and manure, its nursing by the rotation of crops, the use of tree and shrub screens for wind breaks and the production of humidity, and much else.

Nutrition includes the economics and resources of good marketing, through which this food reaches the consumer as fresh and intact as to its potential factors as the produce can be considered to supply; the art of its preparation, cooking, and presentation; and its biological values in terms of nourishment and energy for human tissues.

The vegetable kingdom grows its tissue structures from mineral substances in the soil, the water that it draws through its roots and gathers through its leaves, and the carbon dioxide in the air. Animals feed and grow on this produce and on smaller animals bred in the same way: fish in their medium follow the same behaviour pattern. Man obtains food for his tissues from all these synthesized organic sources.

The housewife, the consumer, is chiefly concerned that the final product, the food served and eaten is attractive and provides the diet requirements for a good standard of health.

Research has established these various daily needs for

39

infancy, childhood, the adolescent, the adult, and the aged, and for different daily activities, both as to quantity and the specific substances the food should contain to promote optimum health.

Detailed knowledge of these dietary factors is of great value. Resistance to disease requires a good standard of health, and it is all too easy to acquire slight or sub-conditions of scurvy (due to lack of sufficient Vitamin C), beri-beri (a polyneuritis caused by a lack of Vitamin B_1), and a tendency to fracture bones (due in part to an unbalance of calcium and Vitamin D factors): coronary and vascular diseases are undoubtedly caused by an unbalance of fats in the diet, and other factors, over many years. These are but several conditions caused by unsuitably balanced diets.

Most foods contain protein, carbohydrate and fat, water, mineral salts and Vitamins, in varying proportions and incidence. Some of these foods are predominantly protein, others consist largely of carbohydrate, and others almost wholly consist of fatty acids or oils. The chief exception is purified sugar which is crystallized carbon and water.

Although proteins, carbohydrates, and fats can be converted into terms of Calorie values, these foods are not interchangeable for nutritional values. Only a combination of these foods, and in suitably balanced proportions supplies body tissues with the essential nutritional factors needed daily. And this is best effected by using a variety of well chosen foods spread over three, or four smaller meals a day, the total for the day providing that day's requirement of nutritional substances.

These *rather general* nutritional balances for each adult person each day can be considered to be—

4–6 ozs protein foods (at least half this being first-class protein).

8 ozs or a little more of carbohydrate foods : say twice

as much carbohydrate as protein, and half of this food should consist of whole grain produce.*

1 oz fat or oil for all purposes and a little cream, a total of 8 ozs per week,

and at least 8 ozs of fruit and vegetable produce; rather more is advisable.

Milk can be taken additionally.

During the digestion of foods, oxygen unites with the particles liberating heat which is converted into energy. Energy used for various body purposes is measured as units or Calories. Individuals have a wide range of Calorie needs. Calories have been converted into terms of food and are—

One gram of carbohydrate is taken as 4 Calories
One gram of protein is taken as 4 Calories
One gram of fat is taken as 9 Calories

The mineral content of food has no energy value, and the comparatively few Calories that vegetables and fruits have are due to the natural sugars and starch content : if, in cooking, some fat or sugar has been added, the Calorie content will be markedly increased.

The importance of protein in food is the amino acids it contains. Proteins after digestion consist of amino acids which are soluble.

Eight of these amino acids are *essential* to man and must be supplied from his diet. Proteins that contain these essential substances are termed first-class proteins. Less valuable protein foods when used in a mixed and varied diet add to the total and make a useful contribution to the needs of body tissues. Thus, wheat or maize *with milk* can give as good *protein* value as meat, and pulses and cereals which are classed as second-class

---

* Some people never eat potatoes, some never eat bread : others find an 85 per cent. loaf or Hovis suits them well : these general figures indicate a desirable balance.

proteins can provide full protein value when supplementing or combining with other foods in a meal.

Good quality milk and eggs provide first-class protein value, particularly for invalid cookery and for young children since, normally, they are easily digested. Protein cheese has high value, then down in the scale come lean beef and fish, soft cheeses, whole grain cereals, pulses and nuts. Cereal proteins with soya beans supplement well : the soya bean needs high temperature cooking.

Lacto-vegetarians easily obtain high-class protein values from milk, cheese, and eggs.

The simplest carbohydrates are sugars : these contain no protein, but combined with cereals or fruit at breakfast provide a quickly utilized source of energy for the day's work. Unrefined sugars have a small mineral content; a good honey will have a minute protein content and some small mineral content; and jams and marmalades should have some Vitamin C content in the fruit. These are therefore considered preferable forms of sweetening.

Carbohydrates which retain their mineral and Vitamin content assist in metabolizing the proteins. Those which are unduly processed, e.g. polished rice and quickly cooked processed oats thus lose their Vitamin B content, and some other item in the meal has to metabolize these products. This leads to an undesirable Calorie intake.

The body depends largely on its intake of carbohydrate and fat for its energy needs. This 'energy' includes not only man's movement of his body and his limbs, but the conduction of nervous energy in the various activities of thinking, writing, talking, cooking, cleaning, gardening, breathing and sleeping, and to maintain body heat—which is continually being lost through the skin pores, the out-breath, and the excretions. As well, all the processes of body metabolism, digestion, the production of cell secretions, the hormones, the enzymes, all ceaselessly use energy.

But too much of the energy foods in the daily diet increases weight: rather less carbohydrate and a little fat gives quicker satisfaction than a high intake of carbohydrate without fat. The carbohydrate eaten with the fats promotes oxidation of the fats.

The body requires some fat content in the daily meals to supply the essential fatty acids. Fats have protective value, particularly when these include Vitamins A, D, and E. Fats are required for digestive purposes, and are constituents of nerve sheaths. Fats yield Calories, and energy, in a less bulky form than carbohydrates, but over a course of years fatty deposits lead to obesity, fatty degeneration of the heart, and arterial occlusions.

Moderation in the intake of food while giving sufficient variety, essential nutrients and first-class protein, promotes continuing good health and maximum mental and physical energy.

Daily food requirements are sometimes based on a given total of Calories.* These are very approximately considered to be—

	Man weighing 11 stone	Woman weighing 8 st. 11 lb.
Sedentary occupations	2,500	2,100
Moderately active	3,000	2,500
Very active	4,000	3,000
Boys 13–15 years	3,200	
Boys 16–18 years	3,800	
Girls 13–15 years	2,800	
Girls 16–20 years	2,400	
Children 4–6 years	1,600	
Children 7–9 years	2,000	
Children 10–12 years	2,500	

If a Calorie guide to the day's food is followed, this

* See appendix, *Food Sense.*

must be properly balanced also as regards the proportionate amounts of protein, carbohydrate and fat intake. The Calorie guide is useful when additional quantities are needed by various members of a family, and when the diet has to be regulated and the number of Calories reduced.

The cooked English breakfast of 1 egg, 2 rashers of bacon, 2 slices of toast, butter and marmalade, and 2 cups of tea or coffee with milk and sugar gives approximately 750 Calories. The other two meals of the day will probably each contain rather more Calories, which with another 100 for the additional two cups of tea or coffee with milk and sugar taken during the day (or other drink), very soon totals 3,000 Calories. An Ovaltine, or similar drink made with milk runs into 200 Calories.*

An average helping of green vegetables and salads gives approximately 20 Calories, but if tomatoes, onions, mushrooms, are fried this will easily add 100 Calories to the 20 Calories for each of these vegetables.

An average helping of breakfast cereal (4–6 tablespoonfuls) carries 100 Calories : wheat germ cereal is much higher, but with this a boiled egg or some fruit, and only one piece of toast will be sufficient breakfast for most women. Fresh raspberries, strawberries, or an eating apple average 30 Calories, but a tablespoonful of dried fruit—raisins and sultanas—gives 100 Calories.

An average helping of steamed fish gives 150 Calories : the same fried or grilled approximates 350. One medium slice of cheddar cheese gives 130 Calories (120 Calories per oz). Cheese omelette with 2 eggs gives 200 Calories : 1 tablespoonful of scrambled egg gives 250, and on 1 round of toast 350.

One medium steak or chop gives 350 Calories, fresh boiled peas—3 tablespoonfuls give 60—and 2 small

* See appendix, *Calorie Guide.*

boiled potatoes give 100; of roast chicken 4 slices or its approximate will give 150 Calories. An average helping of fruit tart gives 300 Calories; steamed pudding 400.*

THE VITAMINS

The nutritional requirements of the human body include those organic food substances known as Vitamins. These are *essential* for its metabolic processes and for its normal growth : they probably act as essential factors in the oxidative processes, and they may all have a connection with cell respiration.

Vitamins soluble in fat are Vitamin A, Vitamin D, and Vitamins E, and K : the water soluble Vitamins are the Vitamin B complex, and Vitamins C, and P.

Vitamin A and its provitamin Carotene, is essential for effecting correct nutritional processes within the body and it has a specific relationship with epithelial tissues and with the pigmentation of the eyes.

A deficiency of this Vitamin in the daily diet results in dermatosis, weakened epithelial tissues—with increased susceptibility to infections not only of the skin and alimentary tract but also of all internal organs, the eyes, and the ears. The eyes, particularly are affected with xerophthalmia, cornification of the retina, and night blindness.

Vitamin A is obtained from a well-balanced diet of eggs, cheese, milk, butter, cream cheese, green and yellow vegetables and fruits, liver, and some fish liver oil (which may have to be taken in capsule form). A liberal daily intake of this Vitamin is advisable at all ages since it is of such great value in building up the body's resistance to disease.

Vitamin D, in association with the parathyroid glands, controls the concentration of calcium and phosphorus in the body fluids and the deposits of both in its bones. It is a factor in forming strong well-formed teeth and bones.

* See Appendix, *Calorie Guide.*

Deficiencies of this Vitamin cause rickets in children and a similar bone condition, osteoporosis, in the elderly : the need for the Vitamin continues throughout life. Adequate supplies of calcium and phosphorus in the daily food, some direct sunlight and Vitamin D foods —egg yolk, butter, whole milk, fresh vegetables, and the fish oils (cod liver oil or halibut liver oil capsules)—these measures should provide the optimum intake. Overdoses of this Vitamin can be harmful : the normal adult probably needs 250 i.u. daily from all sources inclusive of capsule supplements, and this allows for the additional direct supply from some sunshine many days of the year.

Prophylactic doses in pregnancy and in childhood, and therapeutic doses under professional advice are of course higher.

Vitamin E is related to the reproductive processes and probably to nervous stability. It is found in the oil of the wheat germ, in butter, milk, green vegetables, and in whole-grain cereals.

Vitamin K has a specific relationship with the normal clotting of the blood. The Vitamin as used by the human body is obtained partly from the food (it is found in green peas and most green vegetables), and partly from bacterial activity in the intestine.

Any deficiency of this Vitamin usually results from defective absorption within the intestine, and can occur from chronic diarrhoea, dysentery, ulcerative colitis, idiopathic steatorrhoea. Spontaneous haemorrhages result from a deficiency of this Vitamin : in surgical treatment its routine administration is recommended by most surgeons.

The Vitamin B complex is a group of Vitamins, chief of which are Vitamin B_1, Vitamin B_2, Vitamin B_6, Vitamin B_{12}, and Nicotinic Acid.

Vitamin B_1 is essential for the maintenance of normal appetite, the correct metabolism of carbohydrates, and the health of the digestive tract. A deficiency causes polyneuritis and impairs normal growth. Good sources of this Vitamin are found in wheat germ and bran, natural un-polished rice, wholemeal flour and coarse cut oatmeal. It is contained also in tomatoes, eggs, yeast, yeast extracts, and green vegetables.

Vitamin B_2, or Riboflavin is another Vitamin essential in nutritional processes. Symptoms of a deficiency are sore mouth, persisting diarrhoea which may be accompanied with nausea and vomiting, a rash that usually occurs on the back of the hands, headache, sleeplessness, depression, and perhaps dizziness. Good contents of this Vitamin are found in yeast, liver, fish, milk, eggs, and green vegetables.

The B_6 Vitamin is also necessary for normal growth. A deficiency usually affects the skin and shows in a dermatitis. Whole-grain cereals, pulses, liver, fish, milk, eggs, lettuce, are the best sources.

Vitamin B_{12}: part of this Vitamin consists of the element cobalt. It has been demonstrated that this Vitamin is an essential factor in preventing pernicious anaemia. It is known to occur in liver, fermentation liquors, and in milk.

Nicotinic acid, or the P.P. Vitamin, is the pellagra-preventive factor. Symptoms of a deficiency of this Vitamin in the food are glossitis and stomatitis, the tongue being swollen with a beefy-red appearance; diarrhoea is usual, and the dermatitis appears on those parts of the body exposed to light; the mentality becomes depressed, confused, and apprehensive, and may worsen to hysteria. This Vitamin is found in liver, yeast, milk, cheese, eggs, and cereals, in association with others of the Vitamin B group.

Vitamin C is essential for correct nutrition, and it promotes the quick healing of wounds and injuries. High intakes are thought to reduce fatty degenerations of the arterial system, and are probably of value in rheumatic and arthritic conditions. A deficiency of this Vitamin produces various degrees of scurvy, the symptoms of which are loss of weight, breathlessness, general weakness, swelling of the gums and loosened teeth, rheumatism-like pains in bones and joints, oedema, small haemorrhages under the skin, tissues bruise easily, degenerative changes in the heart, and general nervousness.

All fresh vegetables are good sources of this Vitamin, and young sprouting leaves, saladings, citrus fruits (oranges, lemons, grapefruit), blackcurrants, strawberries, gooseberries, loganberries, tomatoes, watercress, freshly-cut cabbage, freshly pulled spring onions, and green, red and yellow peppers.

Heating, drying, pasteurization, usually destroys the Vitamin, as also grating, bruising, pounding, and much cutting of the vegetable and fruit tissues : the produce is best eaten very fresh and handled as little as is reasonable.

Vitamin P is associated with Vitamin C as a nutritional factor. It controls the permeability of blood capillaries, which without the presence of this Vitamin allow the blood to seep through into surrounding tissues with the effect of bruising. This Vitamin apparently prevents *small* haemorrhages from capillary structures. Vitamin P quickly clears the scurvy symptom of small patches of blood underneath the skin which do not respond to an intake of Vitamin C.

Vitamin P is found in leaf vegetables, in blackcurrants, cabbage, lettuce, tomatoes, cherries, apples, plums.

TWELVE TISSUE SALTS USED IN NUTRITIONAL THERAPY

Elements compound into very many chemical forms, of which the salts constitute a very large number of combinations, and these include most inorganic compounds.

The importance in the human body of the inorganic salts in maintaining healthy metabolism has been known now for over a hundred years. Their use as a natural form of nutritional therapy was pioneered by Dr. Schüssler and later by Dr. Julius Hensell who made extensive studies in this field and developed the scope of these micro-nutrients.

Twelve Tissue Salts were first postulated, matching the then known analysis of the blood, and were used with considerable success. These salts have specific relationships with human tissues, body fluids, and function, and continue to be used as nutrient-remedies. They are each first triturated to give very fine dilutions of various exact calculations, called the potencies, and compressed into cellule form in a sugar of milk medium for convenient handling.

In the body fluids these constituent salts immediately ionize and effect the desired normal (though minute) chemical activities. Such chemical activity instigates conduction within the cell and brings the tissue to normal vitality.

This nutritional therapy has found many practising adherents in Germany, America, Great Britain, and many parts of the world.

Advances in laboratory technique have made it in-

49

creasingly possible to understand the behaviour patterns of major chemical elements and of trace elements, and to detect and evaluate their functions in human tissues. Research has detected and demonstrated the effects of chemical unbalances in tissues and related these to sub-normal health and major disease, including the severe effects of certain minute deficiencies in plants, animals, and man. These dietetic factors and factors of meta-bolism include the inorganic elements, Vitamins, hor-mones, enzymes, and other minute substances.

It is very much easier to demonstrate laboratory provings than show the same results in living tissues, especially human tissues. In the latter there are com-plicated emotional and mental factors : neither can the activities of certain enzymes and hormones be entirely eliminated at will from living tissues in order to make a demonstration of one or another factor. But having carefully considered all the known factors, certain nutri-tional therapy is advised and a healthy condition is then effected, some part at least in achieving this can be claimed for that nutritional therapy. The living organism has been able to heal itself because some minute sub-stance previously deficient has been supplied.

In long-standing chronic conditions of disease—because of consequent debility and loss of cell vitality—the constituent salt will most probably require the presence also of its relevant catalyst or other pertinent factor to effect the chemical activity within the cell, or tissue. These *compound micro-nutrients,* having been finely triturated to mathematical formula, are obtain-able* prepared in the one cellule, and should be used for specific and more difficult conditions of diseased tissues.

When using the nutrient Twelve Tissue Salts, several rather than only one Tissue Salt may be needed. Thus, a strained muscle which is also badly inflamed, requires

* See Appendix.

nutrient doses of calcium fluoride *and* ferrum phosphate
—and of course the injured part should be rested.

The Twelve Tissue Salts are listed as—

Calcium Fluoride	Calc Fluor
Calcium Phosphate	Calc Phos
Calcium Sulphate	Calc Sulph
Ferrum Phosphate	Ferr Phos
Potassium Chloride	Kali Mur
Potassium Phosphate	Kali Phos
Potassium Sulphate	Kali Sulph
Magnesium Phosphate	Mag Phos
Sodium Chloride	Nat Mur
Sodium Phosphate	Nat Phos
Sodium Sulphate	Nat Sulph
Silica	Silica

SOME USES FOR EACH OF THE TWELVE TISSUE SALTS

Calcium Fluoride

This salt influences the elasticity, the tone, of connective tissues, including muscle cells and the structural cells
of glands. When such tissue is flabby, or glands become
enlarged, or the elasticity of muscles has been strained
(resulting in a strain or sprain), the presence of this salt
in the blood and fluids of the body will be utilized at
such sites to restore normality.

The calcium and the fluorine are ingested in the daily
food and drink in compounds of organic and inorganic
matter. These are broken down in the processes of metabolism and variously utilized: the inorganic substances
reform as salts in the body fluids and are, or should be,
available for such repair work.

If such conditions become chronic, indicating a fault
in metabolism, specific intakes of this salt *in high dilution*
should prove corrective.

This tissue salt is used in nutritional therapy for

varicosity, enlarged glands, enlarged lymphatic vessels, muscle strain, torn ligaments, prolapsed tissue, hernias.

In contrast, another form of inelasticity shows itself in tissue indurations, in hardened glands, tumours of the breast, hard styes, gumboils, lumpy exudations affecting bone tissue, callosities, ganglion.

Where constipation is caused by a *relaxed* bowel, this salt is needed (indicated by lack of power to expel stools —but also refer to silica). Mitral valvular disease of the heart will need this salt as a trace element combined with other specific micro-nutrients. During pregnancy, for elasticity of the muscles to promote easy delivery, a minute amount of this salt is advised.

If this tissue salt is being given to clear gumboils, and because of the influence potassium chloride has for alveolar tissue, this second salt should also be included in the nutrient treatment; callosities will probably require both potassium chloride and silica as well as the basic calcium fluoride; ganglion will need the addition of potassium chloride to the basic calcium fluoride because of the swollen condition of the connective tissue involved.

This tissue salt is needed where the tissue has relaxed into a condition of haemorrhoids, or piles, together with potassium sulphate if there is much irritation.

Calcium Phosphate

This salt is laid down in the body to form the skeletal bones, but a small percentage also circulates in the blood and is a factor in the process of clotting; this salt is also a constituent of the gastric juice. Its use in the body is controlled by the parathyroid glands: if insufficient is circulating in the blood, calcium phosphate will be drawn from the bones to supply it.

Calcium levels, especially in the elderly, are often too low: bones easily fracture and are slow to heal. The rheumatic-like pains in muscles and even in the joints are partly attributable to calcium deficiency or its *poor assimilation* from lack of sunshine and Vitamin D, to some degree of ageing of the parathyroids, and to a lessening of hormone secretion.

If infants and children have teething difficulties —bringing crying and loss of sleep—with inflamed gums, aching ears or jaws, calcium phosphate (together with potassium phosphate and sodium phosphate), or a specific preparation combining these physiological salts, should quickly ease the condition and allow normal sleep.

Diseases of bones need this tissue salt as a micronutrient together with graded doses of sunshine or ultraviolet light, e.g. rickets, osteomalacia, osteitis : pyorrhea and dental necrosis of the alveola, caries of bone and teeth, bone cysts, also indicate a need for this micronutrient.

Excessive appetite may indicate a need for this salt, occasioned by its insufficiency in gastric secretions with consequent lack of 'tone'.

Synovial fluid and bursae should contain this salt and *chronic* bursitis indicates a need for it. Children having a tendency to bronchitis need this salt, and those with adenoids. In addition, they will need potassium chloride and silica.* (Other health measures which control the intake of cooked milk and include specific breathing exercises to promote nasal breathing are necessary to clear these conditions.)

Micro-nutrients with a calcium phosphate base are needed for all enlarged glands, such as tonsils, goitre, tumours, fibroids, polypi; night sweats with debility and chronic cough—particularly if accompanied with expectorations which are greenish and resemble pus; for enlargement of testicles; prostate conditions; ovarian cysts. Such conditions also require calcium fluorine, and silica, and usually respond better to specific combinations

* See appendix for reference to compound micro-nutrients.

of these salts which contain also the relative trace
elements and/or the specific glandular elements which
influence metabolism within these tissues.*

This tissue salt should also be taken with potassium
phosphate in mental exhaustion from overwork, anxiety,
worry; when suffering from despondency and fear;
where there is loss of memory, and the feeling of having
a tired brain; if there is general antipathy to friends; and
in chronic neuritis, and ataxia, when the diet should
contain very little common salt and should include a
really good intake of Vitamins.

In all hypersensitive conditions a combination of calcium phosphate, potassium phosphate and potassium sulphate, should appreciably lessen the intensive nervous
stimuli and thus normalize the body's chemical activities
in response to such reactions.

Calcium Sulphate
The salt formed by the compound calcium and sulphur
is used in biochemic nutrient-therapy to promote healing
where this is slow and there is much degeneration of
tissue. The calcium is a *tissue builder* and is laid down
at such depleted sites, attracting to itself other natural
constituents of these cells and intercellular structures.

The sulphur has antiseptic properties, and has an
affinity for nerve tissue—clearing excessive nerve irritation where this is an accompanying factor of diseased
tissue : sulphur is a constituent of skin and mucous membrane, and the salt will ionize the cell contents of these
tissues to receive repair substances.

Persisting suppuration needs this salt, seen in varicose
ulcers, boils and carbuncles that do not heal, and all
ulcerations that continue to ooze fluid when new tissue
should be forming.

Ferrum Phosphate
The body's first reaction to chilling, infection, and injury
    * See appendix for reference to compound micro-nutrients.

is inflammation. This emergency measure concentrates specific blood substances at the site for healing, and makes additional demands on the iron and oxygen in the blood.

Iron, in the form of the salt ferrum phosphate should be given promptly in all first stage inflammations. A carrier of oxygen, it promotes oxidation at the site, reducing the secondary effects of inflammation by promoting re-absorption and elimination.

Chilling, shivering with soaring temperature, sore throats (if used promptly), strains and sprains, tearing of muscles (with rest of the injured tissue), congestive headache, throbbing of tissue, these first stage conditions need ferrum phosphate.

Redness, soreness, rash, these are first signs of inflammation. If children run into feverishness, they need this salt, together with potassium phosphate and silica;* and only cool fluids to drink. (If they want at this time to eat, then the trouble is most likely purely emotional.)

Inflammatory rheumatism, with redness, swelling, and pain mostly in joints, will need this salt, potassium chloride, and the relative trace elements of lithium and aurum (gold) to act as catalysts: the aurum has to be very finely calculated.†

Potassium Chloride

A second-stage inflammation means that tissues have been invaded a little deeper with pathological substances. The consequent congestion and disturbance of function results in swelling, and an increase in mucous secretions which become thick and heavy with pathogenic material. There is usually aching pain.

Such a condition is seen in swollen glands, in the second stage of nasal infections and chills if thick mucous

* To clear nerve sheaths of irritant or toxic substances.

† See specific compound micro-nutrients.

runs freely, in catarrhal conditions with greyish white sticky mucous, and in soft swellings of soft tissues.

Other predominantly catarrhal conditions as leucorrhea of the vagina (using also sodium phosphate), menorrhagia with clotted menses, and membranous menses, should clear if given potassium chloride. Catarrhal deafness of an acute nature should clear if given this nutrient salt, but a chronic long-standing catarrhal deafness should also be given silica. Deafness due to other causes needs different treatment.

If fatty foods and pastry cause indigestion and diarrhoea (or constipation because the liver is congested), this tissue salt should correct the unbalance present in the salivary and the gastric secretions.

Potassium Phosphate

This salt has specific nutrient affinity for nerve tissue, and for the nuclei of nerve cells.

It is of great use in nerve fatigue due to over-stimulation from overwork and long hours of concentration. The hypersensitive and conscientious need this salt (together with silica) to restore nervous equilibrium.

Mental inertia probably needs this salt (with other health measures); continued anxiety and stress; mental depression; these conditions need this nutrient salt allied with physical exercise, fresh air, and some change of scene. In the older age groups this salt will need to be linked with specific trace elements to catalyse it within the tissues, and depending whether better oxidation is required or some sedation of nervous stress.

Insomnia may need this nutrient salt, but the cause should be considered and whether it is primarily emotional, digestive, or from over-fatigue, since these conditions have different chemical and functional reactions in the body and involve different nutrient salts and various trace elements. (E.g. bromide is a trace element and has a lightly sedative effect when finely triturated, used as a micro-nutrient and linked correctly with potassium phosphate.)

Meticulously prepared triturations to exact mathematical formula of specific combinations of tissue salts and trace elements are micro-nutrients; they are not habit-forming: best results are obtained by the inclusion of general health measures and a suitable diet.

Potassium Sulphate

This micro-nutrient salt is related specifically to cell contents. Sulphur is a constituent of the mucin secreted by membranous cells, and this tissue salt is needed in third degree inflammations—seen in catarrhal conditions with heavy, thick yellow mucous. Skin conditions which heal in part with thick, yellow crusts and then break out again and again, usually accompanied with much irritation, bleeding, and yellow pus need this tissue salt. The potassium sulphate should re-establish healthy conditions. (In the skin condition of psoriasis, emotive factors may also be involved: these will need understanding and clearance as well as giving micro-nutrients for the specific skin condition.)

The sulphur of this compound promotes oxidation, and this salt should ease and control certain menopausal disturbances of metabolism. These cause in some women periodic flushing with heavy sweating. If this becomes extensive or chronic a specific micro-nutrient combination of trace elements and sulphates does adjust the metabolism very delicately with marked beneficial results.

To promote oxidation when troubled with a congestive headache *on top of the head*, or with suffocating feelings when in warm rooms, this tissue salt—together with phosphate of iron—should improve the blood circulation and clear the condition.

Sulphur is a constituent of cartilage, and troublesome rheumatic joints—if worse from being warm in bed, or towards evening in hot rooms—should be eased by taking this nutrient salt. In this connection, *chronic* conditions are likely to need a specific trace element combination and gentle-movement-exercises.

Magnesium Phosphate

Magnesium ions balance the calcium ions to control the heart's beat, magnesium being the relaxant factor to the contracting calcium.

This salt has an affinity for motor nerves and muscle tissue. Sharp, shooting or boring-like pain indicates the need for this nutrient-tissue salt. Spasms of bladder, convulsions, contracted tissue; neuralgias, paralysis, palsy, and ataxias; these conditions need this micro-nutrient as the *basic* salt: warmth, or the tissue salt taken in hot water, is additionally effective.

Spasmodic palpitations, flatulence, gastritis, dyspepsia, colic, nervous asthma, stammering, angina pectoris, shivering fits, insomnia with limb weariness and limb jerks, and biliousness or vomiting from spasm of the solar plexus—which feels as though a cricket ball had hit the stomach and taken away the appetite: these conditions need this nutrient salt to improve the natural stimuli of the motor nerves and so regulate and clear metabolic congestion.

Sodium Chloride

This is considered to be the most important salt in the body since it controls the degree and movement of water in all its fluids and tissues. This salt conducts water *to* the tissue cells and by the process of osmosis is there used as required.

If there is a deficiency of this salt in the cells the intercellular spaces become water-logged, seen in such conditions as excess saliva, watery eyes, oedema of tissues, watery catarrhs, vomiting of watery mucous, clear running water from nasal membranes as in hay-fever (which additionally needs arsenicum and sodium sulphate), and in watery skin vesicles.

This unbalance in metabolism shows itself also in excessively dry tissues, as dry scalp with loss of hair, in chronic constipation due to dry stools, in dry and cracked finger tips.

After severe vomiting or diarrhoea, this salt should be taken to restore the sodium balance; where there is constriction of the heart, a rapid and palpitating pulse, collapse of circulation; and if the extremities—the feet, hands, nose—are persistently cold due to too much of a coarse salt in the food which the body tissues have been unable to utilize.

If oedema of the tissues persists, indicating the presence of too much sodium thus causing them to hold on to additional water (other organic functions of heart and kidney being normal), a salt of potassium can be substituted in the diet for the usual table salt (sodium chloride).*

Sodium Phosphate

This salt assists digestion, having an emulsifying action on the fats, which without its presence would inhibit gastric secretion. It also has a catalytic effect on lactic acid accumulation, which is a degenerative process, resolving this into carbonic acid (subsequently to be given off by the lungs) and water.

Sodium phosphate promotes the integrity of the bile and is needed whenever fatty foods cause digestive trouble (but see also potassium chloride in this connection). This tissue salt should clear biliary colic, bilious headaches, and jaundice where the condition of the bile is at fault. Uric acid deposits causing inflammatory rheumatism need this salt to draw the uric acid back into the blood for subsequent elimination. Glandular swell-

* See Appendix.

ings and swelling of the lymphatics due to fat deposits need this nutrient salt in an attempt to emulsify them.

Acute conditions respond well to this nutrient salt, but where chronic indurations have been laid down as seen in the elderly, silica should be tried and gentle massage given daily of the affected joints, using suitable oils or a good analgesic cream to alleviate pain.

This salt is excellent to clear incontinence of urine *due to acidity*, and atony of the bladder from the same cause; cream-coloured discharges with sour odour, sour breath, sour gastric eructations, sour vomit (from infants, children, and adults); sick headaches with giddiness; acid taste; catarrh of thick cream-coloured mucous; tongue coated bright yellow, or very moist; nausea and loss of appetite; legs feeling weak and usually accompanied with rheumatic pains in joints or feet; skin eruptions with irritation and honey-coloured secretions; these conditions are all related to an accumulation of lactic acid in the tissues which indicate a need for this tissue salt.

Sodium Sulphate

Sodium sulphate is a constituent of the intercellular tissues and attracts to itself water from decomposition products, assisting the elimination, and thus promoting the further disintegration of waste products. It is needed in dropsical conditions with or after the use of sodium phosphate.

Sodium sulphate has a stimulating effect on tissues of the pancreas and the bile ducts, and is needed in biliousness and diabetic conditions.

Flatulent colic should be cleared with this salt (together with magnesium phosphate) and the low fever of influenza with aching in all limbs. Vomiting and diarrhoea *with much bile*, skin eruptions with greenishyellow or green mucous, tenderness over the liver from congestion and neuralgias, oedemas and particularly of feet and ankles, agglutination of eyelids, ringing noises in the ears, bronchial asthma (requiring also arsenicum and other trace elements), dropsy from kidney disorder, distended stomach and soapy taste in the mouth, ataxia (using also magnesium phosphate and silica): these are some of the conditions that need this nutrient salt.

Silica

This salt is a constituent of all connective tissue, the hair, the nails, and the skin, and the health of these tissues is protective of underlying structures, that of the brain, the spinal cord, all nerve tissue, muscles, and organs.

Silica promotes the elimination of pus, and attracts the absorption of effused blood for elimination.

Silica promotes natural perspiration where this is insufficient, restoring to the skin its normal eliminative function, and this nutrient salt can be used to promote suppuration of *external* abscesses. It would be most unwise, though, to use this salt for internal suppurations of the appendix or mastoid, which would be very difficult to control: these are *very serious* conditions which should have had earlier attention, clearing them before such conditions go on to suppuration.

This tissue salt is needed by the older person who easily becomes physically tired and especially if this is associated with nervous irritation, with sensitiveness to noise; in taciturnity; if body-sweat is foetid or if stools are foetid; for constipation due to partial expulsion and recession of stools; and for headaches from overstudy or mental exhaustion (with potassium phosphate).

Other conditions needing this salt are congestion of the lachrymal ducts, persistent styes, ciliary neuralgia, and deafness from uncleared catarrh. Caries of bones (which also needs calcium phosphate and good Vitamin intake), ulcerations of the skin (together with additional Vitamins A and C), asthma due to inhalation of dust particles, rheumatic concretions, and all third-stage *purulent* discharges to promote clearance of toxic matter, all these conditions need this nutrient salt.

And painful breasts, cracked nipples, sore feet which also feel terribly tender, whitlows, and diseased nails if these are ingrowing or are ribbed, brittle, having white spots, these conditions indicate a need for silica. An irritating, tickling cough needs both silica and magnesium phosphate.

APPENDIX AND BIBLIOGRAPHY

Fundamentals of Chemistry, L. J. Bogert, W. B. Saunders Co., London.

Anatomy and Physiology, Kimber, Gray, and Stackpole, The Macmillan Co., New York.

Manual of Nutrition, H.M.S.O., London.

Food Sense, Edit. Prof. V. H. Mottram, Ward Lock & Co., London and Melbourne.

Calorie Guide, Jane Colin, Arlington Books, London.

How to Use the Twelve Tissue Salts, Esther Chapman, Thorsons, London.

The Twelve Tissue Salts are obtainable, separately, from Homeopathic Chemists, Health Stores, and the British Biochemic Association.

Specific Biochemic Micro-nutrients are obtainable from the British Biochemic Association, Grantham, Lincs., and London, W.1.